To find their way, together

Poems By
Michael Waltz

ISBN: 9781958471050
Contact - waltzpoems@gmail.com
artworkbyaita@gmail.com

The book is dedicated to my mother,
Mary Waltz.

With love to my wife and muse Amy Waltz,
my sons Gage and Bennet.

To my father Jack Waltz, sister Annie,
brothers John, Rich and Tom.
I love you

Special thanks to all of those that inspired and helped to bring this collection of poems to life.
To Aita Gueye for trusting and sharing her lovely painted images with me.

Joanne Allred, Susan Browne, Susan Woolridge,
Brian Gleason, Frank Weitl, Cooki Telles.
Jolene Church Haws and Jim McNeely
And all of my friends, teachers and Chico Poets
that encouraged me on.

Thanks especially to Gary Thompson for his years of friendship, guidance and mentorship.

Contents

III

Foreword: *To find their way, together*

Mike began taking poetry writing classes from me in 1990 at the suggestion of his teacher, Susan Browne, who had been a student of mine several years earlier. Mike, a drummer, was soon joined by other musicians who were revitalizing the Chico music scene, and in one memorable poetry class, at least a third of the students were musicians. We decided to devote one session a week to talking about the differences and many similarities between song lyrics and lyric poems. We learned that for most lyric poets, language is, first and foremost, sound and they make the language *sing* all by itself with various beats, rhythms, and an infinity of vowel and consonant melodies, much as skilled musicians do with their instruments. Mike called the group "our little class of troubadours," and recently commented, "To develop the ability as musicians and artists to write lyrics is a profound advantage when you can do it well. To be poets."

As you will soon discover, the title of this collection comes from the first poem, a richly drawn, dream-like vision about migrating geese caught and grounded by a terrifying storm in the night, where at least one of the flock is killed by a predator. The remainder of the flock naturally must stay together to survive, to find their way north. But the poem gets more interesting as we consider the couple experiencing the same storm as it drives them "further down/ beneath our covers/ together under each crescendo." And as the frantic calling of the lost and circling geese "pulls us back awake/ like our son's voice/ at our bedroom door," we sense that the title line applies equally well to the family in the poem, that they too must hold together to find their way. This theme, or some variation on it, runs throughout the collection, from the fascinating and moving poems about his childhood and his mother and father, through the love poems in the second section, and all the way to the last poem, "the wind and the dark." In this poem, the speaker has long been haunted by the traumatic death of a nine-year-old boy in the ER where he worked. He tries coping with the troubled memories of the boy's death by grouping it with those of relatives who died more expected and natural deaths, but in this he is only partially successful, and this ambiguous state is nicely captured in the final image: "the dark just beyond my open door/ a wind just calm enough to close it."

Mike began sending me drafts of poems for comments and suggestions about three years ago, and most of the poems in this collection were written since that time. However, several of the love poems date back to the 90s when our troubadours still roamed the campus. Together, these thirty one poems sing of Mike's life, and for a beautiful example of that singing, you might read aloud the first stanza of "blue oaks" slowly and with a brief pause at the end of each line—that's *singing!*

—Gary Thompson

I

and what remained

I.
from our bed
we hear it begin.
far out in the distant air
a rush gaining speed
balling up like a clenched fist that
breaks over us
in a shattering thump
driving us further down
beneath our covers
together under each crescendo.

we imagine back
to when waves would have rolled wild over this place.
a wind that caressed them
like hands
and lips of a feverous lover
until dream and sleep submerge us.
calm arrives
touching the seafoam
smooth in the hissing remains
of currents dying out.

and on our horizon
distant cries
wayward answers sounding out
to stay together
to find their way, together.

II.
I have stood on the hillside before
in the fog of spring and heard them.
surprised with the sudden rushing of a tired flock
cutting through air

almost as one bird.
quiet parting of the mist
so low on the treetops
I could hear the labored breathing.
but tonight, it is the calling
a gravity that pulls us back awake
like our son's voice
at our bedroom door.
echoes from the night's deep walls
drifting in on the calm mercied breeze
lost and circling above us.

when in the morning
tide receded
I walked out to the fields and saw
white feathers in the rocks
wings still stretched as if in flight
and the cold palette of green moss and lichen
framing the silk down
pulled aside
the red wound still bright
a taken life and what remained.

did they know
as all things must someday know
the price and balance measured out
delivered to the hungry eyes
and waiting teeth
that caught them in that sudden struggle
among the buck brush.

did they take to flight blindly
and rush into the sky
rising up and gathering together
again, to find their way north.
did they circle back
sounding out the call

until they knew
as all must know
how cries become thank you
                    in the circle growing
                                        and farther on
                                                    become goodbye.

over water

I met her when winter rose up on the wind
the dark sky arriving
as it fell
I watched her run.
and passion swelled the banks
swallowed the saplings
and cut into the places
desire yearns to wander.
she pulled me
to watch rich and rushing waves glisten and roll hypnotic
and chase her along the shallows
to the bridge where we first kissed until
she rolled beneath me and away
as lovers will.

flowers in February start to show
that she is everything.
a mist to gently trace fingertips across my neck
or the frost that shines quietly in the morning hours
turning her muddy fever clear.
crystal glides over the river rock
like some secret treasure heart
inside her chest.

or drifting in June
how, dancing with abandon
she hides and shows between the rocks
currents and turns
still cool from the lingering mountain snows.
enough to seduce the skinny dippers
who surrender
and again
the soft eddy
spins them like a newfound love

and released
to dry themselves
on her shoreline under the sun.

and then brackish with moss in late summer
lying still with the water walkers
scattering her reflections of clouds and branches.
finished with the swimmers
giving what is left of her
comfort to seep into the roots
sun drunk and sleepy
in the late hours of the season.

and when the creek bed sits dry
I go down to the bottom
a stone that longs to be turned to sand
between the channeled soil and the hanging bare root walls.
and I lie down
with my ear to the bottom
and hear her still running
in the dark
soft places of my heart.

falling green

trees turn slightly
around halfway
and leaning to the ground
as they finally fall down.
green trees fall differently
somehow animated and relaxing
they hold on
until the gentle rushing of
leaves and branch
is silent.
others break halfway
leaving ends
lightning struck and charred.
and some trees die all their lives.
I hope I fall green
living to the last
turning
and with a great sigh lie crumbling down.

blue oaks

walk out
into golden summer fields
and stand in the shadows of oak trees.
there are those
with branches that sway low
down into the waves of tall grass.
hands along the tide
as it sways in
and out again.

fall asleep under canopies
watch the sky
filter above the twisted dance of arms
blue to purple
to red
to stars.

see the lightning scars
left on the grey wood
laid bare and charred.
or the letters cut
by a lover's blade
so many years past.

watch the red tail hawks
cruise invisible currents
casting great shadows down
on a slow glide
between the trees.
or songbirds
flashing colors
as they fly.

wonder how in growing

some branches turned
and chased love
perhaps to the sky and found
the sun.
the old stand together
with the saplings just beginning
incarnated again and again
and again.

sit with them to
touch the breeze
to know the light and
the moon.
if for just one brief glance
at the blue oaks, lives seeming still
as they wade into the golden tide
fingers along the crest
as it breaks
each day.

morning prayer

to those who ran into the storm
took tired hands
and panicked hearts
carried them from dark to light
flame and ember to clear blue morning sky.
we rise.

to those that stayed and gathered up
what life remained
that reached out
and pulled together
in those crystal moments of fear
to save another.
we rise.

and you took us in
soothed the burns and eased
the shock
still fresh and bitter in our eyes.
you fed and clothed my children
your children
our children.
my God the children.

to lift each other up
from ashes
and grief
the cold emptiness of loss
to the soft loving arms of a home.

together.
we heal.
we rise.

for Paradise

after the fires

above the old rock walls
next to the creek
a great horned owl holds communion.

the wildfires had burned for months
a hazed sky
had choked the world in ashes.
early on the first smokeless morning
I set out down the mountain to town.

I wheeled onto Cohasset road
the newborn colors rising
from the ridgeline
to the east
as night faded low in the sky.

on the telephone wire a shadow
left my heart quieted
shivering in some deep forgotten way
a field mouse caught in the open grass
eyes wide.
waiting.

the moment slowed as I recognized
the horned head
leaving me and turning back to the hatchling sky
my trespass forgiven.

a perfect silhouette between my eyes and the blue
pink and amber tendrils
following the remnant smoke heaven bound.
ghosts of forests and grasslands
souls interrupted
hanging still

in fragile and glorious light.
deep in the spell
collecting omens or
delivering your death
gathered as you have forever
to another world
on silent feathers.

or were you thankful
like me
just to see the horizon again
and to have once more
a direction to fly.

messages of cooler days
put summer's endless furnace to rest.
and rains to sweep aside the flames
as a mother's hand calms a riotous child
whispering
"enough now, quiet now".

I left the vision there
as I had found it.

a haunting prayer
between messenger and spirit
harbinger and muse
a soft scene of reverence
better left to
drink its secrets
as the ancient gates of dawn swing open
slowly coming to life.

above the old rock walls
next to the creek
a great horned owl holds his communion.

- *for Linda Thompson*

dad's move

the model train tracks spill out
just above the concrete
from the file box.
the failed
splintering of what was never meant
to hold together.

now the heaped piles
trail back along the garden wall
of cowboy shirts and silk ties
ancient coffee cans half full of abandoned
tools rusted and dull
that once filled his hands with purpose and solution
to what was broken and incomplete
now can't fix any of this.

there is still an echo
of ruin and regret
fading under the blanket of a quiet California afternoon.
the estate sale van
lingers at the bottom of the driveway
like a buzzard stepping
closer in.

a man sits nearby
in the faded fabric chair
his drink quietly sweating a ring
in the gorgeous antique table.

gazing a lifetime away.

all the painted horses

morning walks down our long road
past the neighboring corrals
where they would stand waiting
ears pricked full forward
stamp and huff
ponies at the approach of the cowboy.
gathered to greet you
a short communion of orchard apples
or a carrot you have brought along
the quiet gaze into the canyonlike eyes
one soul regarding another.

you taught me very young
to trust my horse
will know the way.

you would tell me that story
how in late October
when you were just a boy
working the pack station out of Green Creek
for Uncle Jay
it must have been the forties
packing in deer hunters
around Yosemite.

you were far back in the wild
late in the fall afternoon
too far to turn around
and farther still to make it home.
the high mountain winds brought the ocean
cold and suddenly
just over Virginia Pass.
a fury of white descended on you
at once erasing

the switchbacks above the tree line
the moraines and
mountain mahogany.
submerged and blinded
and alone
the dark cold closed around you.

you were, you said
the most scared you had ever been.
you pissed yourself in the saddle to stay warm
as all turned dark
and winter crashed down.
too cold to clutch the reins
to save your hands
you let go.
and the horse beneath you
as if seeing beyond this world
painted each step through the drifts
down the mountain trail
to the cabin and the waiting corrals
at the bottom of Dunderberg Canyon.

"trust your horse", you said
"the horse will know the way home".

that was your way with them.
a better cowboy than a husband
or a father.

David Grant Memorial Hospital.
I had my list
and carried these things all the way to the door.
the confusion of divorce to an 8 year old boy
the resignation you left for us
and all the times I was lost
trying to find a way
without you.

we sat for five nights together
in blue mersa gowns and gloves
to reconcile
all that had and had not been
and to say goodbye.

far from the barns and fences
and your kindred spirits
your soul's repeated surrender
still tethered to the infection
embers warm under ashes.

in the end forgiveness comes easy.
it's an old friend arriving
a soft hand
quieting a fever.
just as the long mountain stream finds a way back
from the ice
to soften the edges
roll between stones
and reveal the gold.
it deepens the places you need to remember
and washes away all the things you don't.
the morphine drips
like the first thaw of spring
as if you were there again
on that rocky pass
in two worlds at once
blinded to the trail.

were you waiting for me
to give back your words
to tell you let go the reins
and trust your horse knows the way home.
to go on ahead
and make camp beside the lake.
there by the fire

in happy amazement at the dream
that melts the snow flowers
all around us.

the drive home from the hospital
took me again past
those painted ponies
kicking at the wild wind
somehow knowing what it carried.

they were beautiful.
running back to the barn
they to theirs, I to mine.

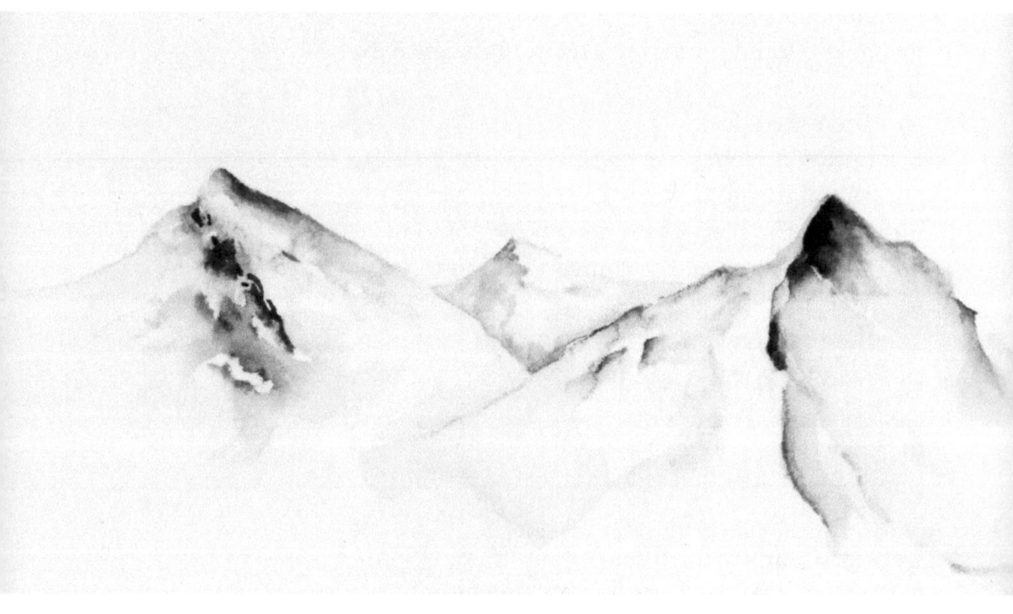

gravity of a wave

they waved me in
to the hospital room
the unexpected gravity
held my feet to the tiles.
a quiet rhythm
of air moving softly
a tired rolling push and the pull
under prayer and whisper.
saying peace
of safe journeys and love.
all love.

later at the house
we talked about
how that gravity of loss softens
the lens.
how all the things we carry
leave us
and the love remains
that pulls us closer.

inhale.
love for our children
remembering their small hands reaching
for us.
the quiet heat
of breath like soft morning sun
evening fireside
pulsing smile
gentle tears
swell under our words
love spoken again
and again.
it is all of us now.

exhale.

happiness pure in thought
we remain
in light.
farewell.
in all
is love.

st. anthony please hear us

the IRS agents arrived
in the morning hours at Woodbridge farm.
there to find my father and exact
the cost of his sins.

through the pantry door
they cut shadows across the hearth
displacing the light suddenly and strange.
finding that Dad had gone
they started in on her.
and on us.

just ten and thirteen, my brother Tom and I were all she had
to stand by and watch from behind the butchers' block
hold the dog and listen
try to understand what was about to happen.

the dish towel still wet
she clutched in her apron
as they sat her down at the kitchen table.
hand reaching across the breakfast plates
words came heavy like shoes on wood planks
right to remain silent
over remnant eggs and toast.

I watched her still herself
as if in prayer.
underneath the noise I could see
her hands open in petition
to find a way for her family.

a lesson I would often forget
to still my mind
when all seemed lost
to turn into a wind that you cannot run from
and find faith.

II

orchard poem

how many poems do you want
are left
are waiting to shine
fall around us
will spread out
take root
find home
wake up within
draw the sky
sleep in until
whisper I love you
remember your smile
sit in the quiet
and follow the dream
to its end.

there won't be any left
when I'm done
out in the orchard
I will pick the trees of every one
from the high branches
where I will climb
unsteady and scared
to even the overripe and soft
on the ground
up from the frost to my cold hands
and put them in my shirt
like a fat man's belly stretched and strained
back to the house
back to you.

and in the stainless pantry sink
we will wash away the dirt and leaves
all the words that we don't say anymore

hold them up
to the window
to each other
bruises and worm holes
naked shimmering
and pure again.

two rivers

morning found us
warm in our sleeping bags
looking skyward to the tranquil cloudless day.
newly washed of darkness
we broke camp and made our way
to where the two rivers met.
you swore that you heard laughter
carried on some breeze
or in the soft warble
of the waters just beyond our path.

and when we found it
the place where fast moving water
came together around the smooth plateau
out on the flat rock
the air relaxed
warm as it held us
naked and wet from the currents.
you with your sly smile
me with your earing
in my teeth.

on the vine

blackberry on the vine
let your sweet way find itself here.
we'll throw out the long planks
deep between the bushes
to reach the ripest fruit.
and fill our hands
with treasures untouched to taste
on our lips.

when it spills out onto the fingers
soaks the skin
staining them red
lust and wanting more.

and the moment took itself
late in the summer
spreading onto the page
like you wide and open
on the picnic blanket.

you took off your dress
and painted yourself with the juice
of each berry.

butterfly

take to the sky
and though brief
live and love the breeze that holds you
delicate in its soft swells.
fold your wing and wait for night
to roll away its shadow.
sip the dew on new blossom silk
and bask in the sunbeam while you can.
I would be either for you
in a dance so lovely that
a thousand poems and daydreams
erupt as flowers beneath us as we go.
and love you to the end of all things.

4 a.m.

elizabeth knows
about moonlight.
the way
in early morning dark
it watches us here
on this river bridge.
she says these words to me
and smiles
as a dream.

we stand
over the whispering
song of rain
while the sky
pulls back its clouded curtains
to give us
light to kiss.

my girlfriend's new bed

she keeps it smooth and tight
as if to hide evidence of the morning
that woke and left it behind.
under the dark oak headboard
the pillows curve down
into the long sloping quilt.

I peel back the lace
and slip into the soft sheets
where she lies
naked and stretching in wait
of my hands and lips.

the sky bruises
until clouds bleed to the roof
and night grows wet
dark and deep.
and we return like dreams
to the new linens.
she turns down the light
and candles throw shadows
of us
on the walls.

there are only stars
left at the edge of our touch.

my lover asks me

for a poem
about the sex we share.
she wants to feel
the words drip quietly
from my warm breath.

it will be
to write and speak
the curve of her legs
coming together where
life waits to awaken.
to profound
the bending into her
to taste instinct in the silk
warm with the pulse of us
a tide taking shore
and retreating.

my lover asks me
as she lies back to let me
write our poem
in soft whispers.

elizabeth the birds are calling

you must with them
fly
far away
I will wait
count stars
and listen to the air
for songs to sweetly
find my ears

room 2411

it's the a.m.
and talk's turned trashy.
hotel walls are thin
they don't keep company
they just echo
the television scenes
until I'm sleeping.

and you were there
on a warm sand walk
free flow wind wavering
the mist under
some central american sun-soaked place.
where native boys watch
your skin move
in the air
down the beach.
you become the emerald surf
hair back slick
and salted with rolling foam.

there is the slow motion

there is the bright shine
cast from wet skin
lips and eyes
that open to me.
I should be here in the aqua green
around your bare hips
as you throw back your hair and rise.

I should be the native boy
his gaze that follows
the foreign girl as she passes
and smiles
shakes loose the sea.

the night cried

down to the dirt
a universe without you.

when it was time
the garden roots began
to reach
deep into their beds
pressing feet
together on the cold nights
to find warmth.
they took into themselves
what the rain had brought.

while quietly above
all the leaves were waiting.

as if the vines that
curled around my window screen
found you lying asleep
and took you
to hold up in the morning air.

a flower
silk and set aglow
and smiling.

a bird just hit the window

the world forgets broken things.
it's too late to truly learn again
to fly.
the air must love you back
must want you
with the same heart it wants
the rain showers
and sun beams.
to hold the morning fog as a lost child found.
wind must love the feather
to dance the ether
and seduce the velvet song
to sing wild and free.

how words want to be calm
and are betrayed
by an urgent tone of panic
and the deep knowing
the instinct
that your sky has left you
liftless and lost and the song
now but a cry.
"come back, don't leave me
please don't leave me."

invisible vapor across the eye
that now clatters away though the autumn leaves.
soft down now still.
out of place on the patio stones
the broken wing
trying to catch the spell again
panicked in the spent magic
of a drowning heart.
lovers are content to leave.
gravity is the heartbreak to hollow bones.

hummingbird

you were sitting this morning
by the open window
as the hummingbird
swept in around you
and tumbled in your hair.
some mysterious spirit
in an emerald flash.
time standing still
stop motion
around the new mysterious flower.
you squealed and gasped at
the touch
of the wings wash
the smell of summer honeysuckle
gentle over your face.
a dream
a trancelike low tremolo
quiet and pulsing soft on your ear.
I am witness
to something sacred here
to how beautiful you are
morning sun lighting the air
eyes closed to hear
whatever secrets this messenger delivers.
your smile and this moment will blur
and my heart will come to
waking up
from a dream to a dream.

III

the waiting room

I guess first impressions are the most profound.
the day we met in the waiting room with everyone else
there to see the girl that I had just "fallen for."
across the aisle you sat in your quiet way
observing the boy.
perhaps it was my curly hair pulled to a neat ponytail
or my brown suede jacket.

it may have also been the roses from the garden
I had brought to give to your granddaughter.
in the awkwardness
as we traded glances and modest smiles
in your calm eyes you were beyond that moment
and were seeing years away.

to the night when the mariachis played
and the lines between dream and life
were blurred by votive flames
and stars above the white linens.

and the hospital
where we would meet again
and together welcome the tiny souls
that even now dance and play before you.

all of this
was there between you and me that day.
it hung like smoke does
drifting just out of reach
the way secrets and dreams often do.

For Alma

a prayer for the traveler

about to embark
the soul in need of soft words
kisses and tears
and a last caress
to let go.

the quiet dream stirs
as a breeze picks up
and waits for a moment
to look back.
a voice you recall
from so long ago
calls to you
from across the stream.
"come over...I'm here."

there will be morning
and the room will be quiet
and bright.

forgot

mom tells the story how she gathered us up
5 kids into the Buick wood-panel station wagon
for a trip to the city.
only to discover on arriving
that they left me alone in my car seat
not even a year old
on the red-square linoleum floor of our kitchen.
we laugh about it now
but I can tell she was horrified.

or the carnival night
in the churn of running children
"time to go!"
watching from under my mask
the last taillights pull away
into the autumn night.
voices and noise flew like a startled flock
until there was no one.
just the sudden quiet.
the only thing to do was hide under the juniper bushes
next to the cafeteria parking lot
and the John Swett Elementary sign
waiting for someone to remember me.
and when I escaped along the pavement
it was scarier under the street lights
at the turn of the valley road
the light ended
and darkness wrapped around me
like the arms of an old friend.
knowing I was hidden, I felt safe within it
counting each step of the miles ahead
to home.
she was horrified again.

dad forgot me too
but his was a choice.
long before I was aware
he was already gone
often enough that I could expect it
and pull a curtain over my heart.
to slow the wearing down
tread on a shoe
cuts into the butchers' block
winters carving of creeks and canyons
casual lies and empty goodbyes.
these things taught my heart to break.
to learn that what should love and stay
forgets.

now mid-life sets in
and sometimes she forgets too.
indifference creeps like vines over our windows
turns away from kisses
adds up to pillows between us when we sleep
and deflated sighs hang.

until we remember
where whispers ran wild like a spring across the years
to taste a name, her name, my name
and a breath and yes and yes.

and when that leaves me
the valley road and the black night wait just beyond.
to cover me
to walk me home.
but I am not that child anymore
and the way home forgets too
all of those things.
the middle-aged man
holding out under the juniper bushes
waiting for headlights.

just for me

it would be nice
to be home.
barefoot in the yard
thumb over the hose end
squinting as the sun
emerges from thunder cells
swollen with spirits.
listening to bluegrass
green grass
smoke ripe in my eyes.
I'll see you in the hammock
swaying naked in the sun
but for your cowboy hat.
something just for me
a picture just for me.

I go here
when the world closes in
and weighs down.
lost is not forgetting the way to go
but more losing how you got here.

the light grip of confusion
like a child's hand
letting go.

the glass sweats in your hand
you smile at me
under the brim
through the dream of it all
a place just for me.

two birds

we need to find a sky
that never has been flown
deep under the soft down
of your wings
I have listened to
your heart beating
it sings a desire to catch
the air and
kiss it

we are rising
with this sun's fire
if we fall
to earth
our colors will join
and become
the blaze
of fading days

dragonfly

so it begins
snow melting
at your touch.
rivers that push
over dry ground
to get closer.

the dragonflies have
come to dance
with you.
emerald bodies that shine
over the glassy
reflection of a sky.

and I have come
to lay down
my heart.
at your feet.

the wild escape

we walked miles of east bay trails
on the wild rolling hills of my youth
where I showed you my secrets.
the hidden pond where I would go as a boy
to catch bluegill and bass in the warm summer waters.
the old path to the high hilltop meadows and lakes
to escape and lie in the afternoon
lost beneath the clouds and sky
while my pony Tootsie would drink and swim.

and wait for me.

there aren't many secrets left now.
places in my heart that you have never been.
when I find them I bring them to you
as a child brings a seashell
newly found in wonder.

30 years together and
as we walk you ask
how it feels.

it is to be
surprised by the shadow of a hawk
down the trail to home perched above us in the ancient oaks.
so close to us that our breath is stilled.
he had surely been watching us, waiting for us to pass.
now discovered, under his gaze
there is a moment
humble and unsure of a feeling so wild and primal
in eyes that have seen a timeless world.
a yearning to be lost in it.
to surrender and follow the wonder
the rushing wings

on a wave of wind to some other world.

to be reborn.
that is how it felt
to fall in love with you.
how every morning
to awaken
and witness this song begin to play again.

a favor

morning do not break
let the air about my windows
hold longer
to that dark fading pale.
underneath it all
under blankets in warm hibernation
my love and i
weave ourselves together.
the quiet of our breathing
does not escape this bed
it is that distant wind of dreams
of sighs floating over
from the other side of sleep
that pushes the sail.

leave us unstirring
to drift the glass of a stormless sea.

plum blossom

Aunt Alice gave you that name.
five petals to the flower
and as many children too
if you don't count the one that didn't make it.
but you always did.
to break yourself first
through the snow drifts
and shock pink and rich
the coming spring
to a sleeping world.

tell me more stories and I'll tell them too.
pour the wine or the whiskey
and share them one more time.

stealing horses in the high meadows
just below the cabin
to ride the day with brother Billy.
of your childhood in Hollywood
swimming in WC Fields pond
running with the Waynes and Disneys
and cutting your hand on the porcelain handle
in Jack Dempsey's bathroom
as the air raid sirens wailed on V-J day.

you were almost discovered by your screen test
with the pre-Rock Hudson
but Grandad wouldn't fix your teeth
and we all know what happened to Rock.
how you were a bass drummer as a girl
and the homecoming queen at Loyola.

tell me about when I was being born that stormy
November night

how I got stuck and the anesthesiologist
climbed over your shoulders
to push on your belly.

teaching me harmonies in the wood panel station wagon
on the front seat watching you for my cues.
dancing in the living room,
showing me how to surrender myself
to rhythm and song.

or that bar fight in Cabo San Lucas
you were laughing when broken glass shimmered
in slow motion dreams
diamonds brilliantly falling over us.
until I grabbed your hand and we ran laughing and amazed.

and as Ophelia dressed in your nightgown for the festival
only to drown in lane 4 of the Forest Hills pool
for our skit
the Shakespearian Olympian.

I can still feel that hug you gave me at the kitchen table
the day Scott Lepak died.

when I went long hair
we smoked refer in the redwood hot tub.
took me to jazzercise
took me to church
taught me to find myself
and hide my tracks.
showed me how to be afraid
and to gather myself for a fight.
to harness my fear like those high meadow horses
and ride it.
to pick up the pieces that matter and mend them
and to forgive myself
through laughter.

winter snow retreats
and I don't know what's to come.
I'll take every story again from the start
and follow the branches
to the end.
to where all things are born again.
and wait for you there.

the wind and the dark

1.
the living room was so quiet
alone after the viewing downtown
at the Connolly and Taylor funeral home.
the old front door blew open from a breeze
and my voice could only call out
to the dark, "Granddad?"
he was wounded in the trenches
and carried it home.
would sit on our brick patio and cry
once the Jack Daniels soaked in.
now he was the wind and the dark.

Aunt Alice wasted away in her double wide
until we drove down to Turlock to get her.
all the way back home that mountain woman
pissed her diaper
took my hand in the county ward and said
"it's so hard Michael,"
and I left her there.

Uncle Tom lost his leg and unraveled like a broken spring.
he was a giant man
Mom bought a size 64 suit at Men's Warehouse
at 6:30 on the morning of his funeral.
she said, "no brother of mine's gonna be buried in sweats."
they barely had a box big enough for him.

Dad pulled out his tubes that tethered him.
mersa gowns and coffee at the end
for 5 days until he glided off
like the leaves
we used to drop from the wooden bridge
turning as they descended
to our reflections
looking back up from the calm creek water.

2.
and the 9 year old brought in from the accident
to the trauma room table.
bright light on hot skin.
    start compressions
press down
and release
from the stool standing above him
my sweat falling on his bare chest
with each push.

I wonder if he was scared like I was
if he could feel us trying.
a pulse and we pause
blood pools in his sockets.
    compressions
it's not working
a nurse's eyes wide and watering above her mask
can only hold his hand.
joints dislodge, shattered limbs give way
to a deep crimson smell
rich and awful.
and the boy comes apart.

this isn't real.
the soft whispers inside me of
don't come back
please don't come back.

3.
as the warm spring morning streams in
the family runs together across the hospital parking lot
to the sliding doors that slowly part.

this is real.
the small body distorted
and smashed.

snap of wet gloves and
a quiet retreat from the wreckage
when they arrive.
his mother cries
and throws herself across her broken child
as if to gather up and put him back together.

her gasp at seeing him
still finds me
across these many years.

that warm morning air
still like creek water
the dark just beyond my open door
a wind just calm enough to close it.

find

your

way

together.